Will It Fit?

by Gail Tuchman and Anne Schreiber
Illustrated by Tony Griego

SCHOLASTIC

Will fit in it?

 will fit.

2

"A fan!" said .

Will the fan fit in it?

The fan and will fit.

3

"A ," said Fox.

Will the fish fit in it?

4

The  and the fan
and will fit.

fish

Fox

5

"Fat ," said .

Will fat fit in it?

6

No.

My Words

* no

it

Ff	**-an**
fat	fan
fit	
flip	
flop	

*new high frequency words